The Balance Procedure
Universal Symbols
Jenny Cox

Privately Printed

2012

Contents

Introduction

The Balance Procedure (TBP) Universal Symbols

TBP is a powerful tool you use on yourself to keep you in balance in all aspects of your life, the unique nine card set are used as a guidance to assist you in this process. Used as part of our daily life it can increase our confidence, increase energy output and maximise potential

This edition is as an accompaniment and follow up to *The Balance Procedure Book* with a full explanation of the TBP enhancer symbol cards. Its purpose is to assist in exploring fully and specifically how the ideas and principles of TBP can be applied usefully in everyday life.

I sincerely hope that I can share my passion and enthusiasm for this unique relaxation procedure I have created, assisted by my husband Alan, and to establish its position within the field of Energy Techniques. TBP is the evolution of my own life, work, spiritual beliefs and practices. As a practitioner and trainer of a variety of therapies for a number of years, it is only natural that my own findings and experiences would lead me to adjusting the ideas and techniques I have studied to relax and balance the mind body and spirit into what I find works best and most efficiently, on a consistent basis; *TBP is relaxation in action.*

The main principle of TBP is we create our reality through thought and imagination, using our emotions as our guidance, using our emotions this way we change our reality attracting all things to us whether they are positive or negative. Reality is our creation 100 per cent of the time and if we acknowledge this then we have the opportunity to create reality conciously, and acknowledge that we are extremely powerful. If we don't know it or don't like it we still create reality, but we do it unconsciously so that we become 'victims' having no power. 'Victim Consciousness' actually robs us of power because we draw more attention to the negative events or circumstances in our lives giving the negativity more power! It is my aim to guide you to release these negative thoughts and emotions which hold you back allowing you to find your own balance and move forward to a fulfilling and more productive life.

Once we are aware of how an external issue mirrors what's going on inside us, we can use TBP to transform those beliefs that are limiting us, therefore allowing us to create to our highest potential. I believe that we are creative all of the time. 'To create' means 'to bring into existence'. Whatever we are thinking and feeling, we cause the world to change, and we bring new forms into existence. To be alive is to create. Using TBP daily balances our energy systems transforming victim mentality or victim consciousness patterns so we can intentionally create to our highest potential.

TBP assists in transforming energy patterns that we have learnt and no longer need using our HEART energy with INTENTION. The unique difference using TBP is there is no need to discuss personal details or revisit past experiences; all we need to observe is 'what is alive in us now'.

It is our intention to take TBP to the world because it combines ancient philosophy with modern quantum science; it's simpler and more intricate than other techniques and can be an essential part of everyone's 'toolbox'. TBP lifts our vibration adding new sparkle to our life and guides us to be and feel more successful in everything we do. TBP is neither a therapy nor a healing – it's not even a treatment. The aim is transformation; individuals often find that after learning the procedure, their lives do change often in quite radical and far-reaching ways. It is neither the procedure itself, nor the practitioner that bring about the results. They are merely catalysts. The life force working inside each person brings about the transformation.

Your True Potential

If we see a difference between where we are and where we want to be, we can consciously change our thoughts to match our grandest vision. This requires self-awareness on all our thoughts and feelings. It involves making choices on a conscious level. This whole process is a massive move towards consciousness.

What we will find if we undertake this challenge is that we've spent half our life unconscious. We have been unaware, on a conscious level, of what we have been choosing in the way of thoughts unless we experience the reflection of them. We often see the aftermath of our choices as things that were done to us, bad luck, or other power-draining patterns. Many of us have refused to take responsibility for the life we have because of our choices.

TBP used on a daily basis can transform limiting thoughts and beliefs. Beliefs are thoughts we think are true about ourselves, others and life. Unfortunately, some of our beliefs are not empowering us. Some beliefs are counterproductive to what we say we want. We need to identify those beliefs, check them for validity, and then change them. Beliefs are thoughts and thoughts can be changed. There are many self-defeating beliefs – the following are some examples:

- I don't have time to do what I want.
- I can't change. This is just the way I am.
- I would be selfish if I focused on my desires.

- People who are optimistic aren't realistic.
- I have to have love, sex, new car, money, etc., to be happy.
- No pain, no gain.
- We have to do some things in this life we don't want to do.
- You can't have your cake and eat it too.
- If my happiness was a priority, I'd be inconsiderate of others.
- It's a dog-eat-dog world out there.

These beliefs, both positive and negative, can create stress in our lives and blocks to our development. Beliefs are thoughts and when we think disturbing thoughts, our energy system becomes disturbed IMMEDIATELY – that is what causes stress and tension in our bodies. Stress and tension slowly build up, and we unconsciously adapt to more and more pressure, while at the same time try to function normally. In moments of PERCEIVED danger our body gets ready to fight or run. Our sympathetic nervous system prepares our body; it shunts our blood to our muscles and increases our blood pressure, heart rate and breathing rate, which helps us cope with stressful situations. It is automatic but it should only be momentary. Many of us live continuously in these 'fight or flight' conditions.

Keeping our guard up all the time puts pressure and strain on our whole body. Eventually our body 'complains' and begins to send signals that something is wrong. Besides physical problems showing up, our attitude wears thin, too. With less energy, enthusiasm, patience and humour, we no longer function at our best. Because we don't feel good anymore and life seems frightening, we're likely to withdraw increasingly from the world. The following list includes some of the ways we disconnect from our stressed emotions by putting attention elsewhere. These behaviours are – or can become destructive and take over our life.

- Eating, not eating, bingeing purging or just worrying about food all the time.
- Sleeping all the time, especially when the rest of the world is awake.

- Too much television or too much internet.
- Thinking about other people's difficulties too often: your families' problems, your friends' problems, your friends' friend's problems, and so on.
- Using drugs to get high, low, sideways or generally detached from your body and your life.
- Wanting to be alone more and more of the time.
- Thinking constantly about anything, like nuclear war, the economy, global warming, starvation,your health, your weight your wrinkles, and even your future.
- Preoccupation with death, suicidal thoughts

When we are experiencing any of these situations we can apply TBP. Life will become easier and easier when we use this technique to slow down, be calm and live more harmoniously.

When our energy systems are in alignment, our thoughts clear as well. The energy system and thought are aligned and the state of one reflects the state of the other.

Understanding Thoughts
and Emotions

Imagination is everything. It is the preview of life's coming attractions.

Albert Einstein

We are what we think. All that we are arises with our thoughts, with our thoughts we make the world

The Buddha

Our thoughts are one of our most powerful assets! Everything we experience in life is the direct result of our thoughts. The ability to control our thoughts will allow us to choose what experiences, people and events we have in our life. We think thousands of thoughts every single day. How can we monitor them all? We can't, but we can attain mastery over the thousands of thoughts streaming through our head each and every day. The key to controlling our thoughts is to simply observe the emotions that comes from the thought.

Different emotions have different vibrational frequencies. Our emotions are indicators of our personal vibrational frequency, and indicate our degree of alignment with Universal Energy and that the better we feel, the more we are allowing this ideal and natural alignment.

Do you remember the children's game HOT and COLD. We would close our eyes and count to ten. A playmate would hide a toy, and when finished counting we would open our eyes and attempt to find the hidden toy. As we started to move towards the toy our friend would say 'you're getting HOTTER, HOTTER!' as you pinpointed the place where it was hidden and discovered the toy. Our emotions are our guidance, that play a similar game EVERY day, but rather than say HOT or COLD, the universe guides us with feelings. Positive feelings mean we're moving towards something that we want, and negative feelings mean we're heading away from what we want. Our emotions are indicators of our vibrational frequency, they indicate our degree of alignment with Universal Energy and that the better we feel, the more we are allowing our alignment with the things we really want. You can see by using the emotional scale below you can quickly identify whether you are in alignment or out of alignment.

The following scale has been adapted from Jerry and Ester Hicks 'Ask and it is Given'.

1. Joy/Knowledge/Freedom/ Love/Appreciation
2. Passion
3. Enthusiasm/Eagerness/ Happiness
4. Positive Expectation/Belief
5. Optimism
6. Hopefulness
7. Contentment
8. Boredom
9. Pessimism
10. Frustration/Irritation/ Impatience
11. 'Overwhelming'
12. Disappointment
13. Doubt
14. Worry
15. Blame
16. Discouragement
17. Anger
18. Revenge
19. Hatred
20. Jealousy
21. Insecurity/Guilt/ Unworthiness
22. Fear/Grief/Depression/ Despair/Powerlessness.

The Enhancer Symbol Cards

The Enhancer Symbol Cards used in TBP have been created as a multidimensional tool to balance our energy systems on all levels. Symbols are the universal language of the unconscious. They assist the mind in understanding when words may miss the mark. Symbols empower us to balance and evolve the potential to become our true, authentic selves and express an inner reality of which we are often unaware.

Geometric Symbols have a power beyond words, carrying a multitude of meanings that speak to mind, body and spirit and challenge us to go beyond the obvious. Symbols are different from signs. Signs point the way, whereas symbols always stand for or represent something more that the immediate meaning. They represent abstract ideas and concepts that may not easily be put into words. We have always used symbols. We cannot do without them as they are hardwired into our minds and bodies.

Geometric Symbols are generally made up of the same three basic forms – the circle – representing inner being, unity and the universe, the triangle – representing standing man with his three parts, body, mind and spirit; and the square representing manifestation of spirit into matter. Also the circle can represents liquid, the triangle gaseous and the square symbolises solid matter.

| The Circle | The Triangle | The Square |

The contour edges of the universe and the spaces between them can be represented by three types of lines:

| Straight line | Curved line | Angled line |

Symbols can give us greater understanding of our abstract universe – old perceptions of form can begin to take on new meaning and interpretation. Form is mostly associated with the left hemisphere of the brain and colour is the right hemisphere of the brain.by putting together colour and form in meaningful sequences, the left and right hemispheres of the brain functioning becomes synchronised enabling the conscious and subconscious to respond as one. When we see colour around us, we see it in given form. Form can 'say' things to us; it is a universal code. The purpose of combining form and colour is to use the maximum message which form and colour can offer.

The nine symbols used with TBP enhancer cards are: the square, the diamond, the upright triangle, the circle, the downward triangle, the opened square, downward pentagram, upright pentagram and spiral. Each expresses its own quality and energy, they are made up of the three basic forms and contour edges. These support the nine colours by relating to their personal qualities and overall characteristics.

The TBP symbol enhancer cards take advantage of this wonderful source of energy and use it with intention to create harmony and enliven our own being, allowing us to create to our full potential.

Cards of any type signify visual communication, and the ability to convey a message spiritually, that's why I've chosen cards as the TBP medium. Each TBP card has a geometric shape, a polarity principle, a colour, a chakra, a number, a zodiac sign, a gemstone, a planet, an element and various physical aspects.

POLARITY Aspect of the Symbol

The polarity principle, masculine and feminine, is built into the human consciousness, thus the vessel form (feminine) has also the star form (masculine) within. Neither has a purpose unless they can actually relate to each other. Where the vessel (feminine) is in balance with the star form (masculine) a harmonious exchange exists between them.

COLOUR Aspect of the Symbol

The power of colour is a part of the natural energy of the universe. It fills our subtle and physical bodies. Colour associations contribute to our earliest consciousness. As we grow older feelings, memories and meanings are attached to experiences of colour and this results in colour becoming a feature of the subconscious. The association of particular colours with a happy, sad, joyous, angry or frightening experience builds up colour preferences. In this way colour has physical, physiological, emotional and spiritual connotations.

Our responses to colour are governed by deep – seated associations which have been either conditioned by our experiences or inherited from the past. Certain phraseology has a cultural bias, for example 'green with envy' 'seeing red' or 'feeling blue'. This tends to indicate an intuitive connection between feelings and colour used to describe the feeling. What is surprising is that responses to colour are surprisingly similar the world over.

CHAKRA Aspect of the Symbol

The chakras are openings for energy to flow into and out of the aura, and therefore exchange energy with the Universal Energy Field. This energy is experienced in terms of seeing, hearing, feeling, sensing and intuition.

Universal Energy is then translated by the chakras into the glands of the endocrine system, so when we 'BALANCE' the chakras', we are, at a physical level BALANCING the glands of the endocrine system. There are eight major Chakras. They are located at the base of the spine (gonads), the abdominal (adrenals), the solar plexus (pancreas), the heart (thymus), the throat (thyroid), the brow (pituitary) the crown of the head (pineal) and the Alta major (hypothalamus). It is important to remember that there are other minor centres in the body. Traditionally the Chakras function and nature are described through symbolic images not through word.

NUMBER Aspect of the Symbol

The science of numbers is a broad subject, the main principle is that reality is constructed mathematically, and that all phenomena are in fact numbers. Therefore they can be used for just about everything in the universe, and by anyone. There are many different areas of our lives and many different numbers which effect each of those areas: family, wealth, health, career. Each number has a meaning and energy vibration of its own. Everything is energy (including us) and everything has its own vibration. Worked out from our date of birth and our age, numbers are a guide or blueprint to our life path. Numbers have always had a magical appeal and significance in many traditions; for example the number one represents the primary appearance of spirit in matter; the number two, masculine and feminine, and procreation; three the trilogy of mind, body spirit; four, the earth and harmony; five, the human self (five pointed star); six, love, dreams and giving; seven the mystic journey, eight, initiation;

nine eternity and indestructibility. The number aspect on the Universal Symbol cards have meaning and energy that can raise our personal vibration; we all have a set of personal numbers. These numbers describe our talents, attitudes and our hearts desires enabling us to evolve and develop in this lifetime. This does not mean that you will need only these numbers, only that they will be more likely to be able to empower when life seems an effort; they will gently put us back in BALANCE and remind us where we need to be. Our personal numbers are worked out from our date of birth, and age; they are a guide or blueprint that holds a unique vibration.

Life Path Number

Our Life Path Number is the number we were born with. To be born into a body is to be born in time. As our life path number is based on our date of birth, it is the most important number of all, as it can never change. It is like a code that we refer to as we go through life. Our life path number tells us what we need to evolve and develop so that we can fulfil our destiny. The word 'destiny' is really the same as destination or 'path'. When we're on our path we're sure to reach our destination. The secret is to find out what that path is, and the first step is to find out our Life path number.

We work out our Life path number by adding all the numbers of our date of birth together until they are reduced to a single digit.

For example my birth date is 4/10/1950.
So I add 4 + 1 + 1 + 9+ 5 = 20
2 is my life path number.

Personal Year

The year we are in at the moment is known as our personal year. We each live in cycles of nine years. Once we know what year we are in and what we are meant to be doing we can use the appropriate TBP card to keep us in alignment. To find out our personal year we write down the full date of our last birthday:

**Example: My last birthday was 4/10/2011.
So I add 4 + 1 + 2 + 1 + 1 = 9**

So, at the time of writing this book, I am in a number 9 personal year. I believe that we have come to Earth to evolve and develop; we are pioneers of the universe. We each have a destiny to fulfil and we each have our blueprint to guide us on our way. If we are not succeeding at the things that we want to experience in this life, it may be that we are not in the correct frequency. One way to get into the correct universal frequency is to know your Life Path Number and to balance it on a daily basis. Once you are in alignment life becomes effortless and simple. Now you have two vital keys to your life:

Our Personal LIFE PATH Number is the 'doing part' of our life. The PERSONAL YEAR shows us a unique 'window of opportunity' in the nine year cycle.

ZODIAC Aspect of the Symbol

The idea of predestination has existed for thousands of years; that we are born for a purpose which is timed so that we can experience the voyage through human experience. 'As above so below' the opening words on the Emerald Tablet of of the 1st century Egyptian Hermes Trismegistos sums up astrologers' belief in the influence on the lives of humankind of the movement of the stars and planets. The Zodiac is symbolic of our relationship with the universe and is divided into twelve signs that represent the whole of human experience. It is important to remember that every person has access to the energies in the universe. This means that we have access to all twelve zodiac signs and can use their energy whenever we need.

GEMSTONE aspect of the Symbol

Gems stones communicate on every level of our energy systems. They lend access to the higher levels of our energy field and can assist in balancing energy at these levels. They can be assist in resolving confusion around manifesting our life purpose. Crystals synchronise the heart with the mind, ensuring our thoughts, words and actions are aligned and in balance. Crystals transform energy flow at all levels aiding inspiration in creating the reality we want.

PLANET Aspect of the Symbol

The planets are carriers of psychic energy, responsible for the uniqueness and dynamism of each individual. They are motivators, impelling us to seek experiences and passively attracting them. They are equivalent to our 'needs' or 'drivers.'

ELEMENT Aspect of the Symbol

The elements reflect our characteristic nature EARTH – understanding value, both in the material and human sense, reliable and dependable, our physical well being and common sense, FIRE – action, great faith in self, enthusiasm and honesty, AIR – a strong emphasis on thought, ideas and intellectual pursuits and communication skills, WATER – our ability to feel and intuitively know, understanding life through our emotions and 'playing our hunches'. ETHER – our spirituality.

PHYSICAL Aspect of the Symbol

The body consists of 60 trillion individual cells, each containing the genetic information for the life and working of the whole body. Each is specialised according to its function, but nevertheless is coded for all jobs. Each is a hologram.

The network of cells respond to the communication of thoughts and are felt by emotions. Some of these are handled with ease others disrupt (anger, fear, discord) and cause negative reaction. Uncertainty and negative thoughts may create demands, which overload the network.

There are subtle changes in enzyme chemistry, which lower the capability of the cells to fight off the bacteria, and germs, which are always present and can allow a state of disease or illness to occur.

The Balance Procedure

I BALANCE all of the cards together daily, but I also use individual ones when I need them. For example, when I am starting a new project, job or something new I BALANCE the red square and turquoise triangle card (Number 1) that empowers me to take the initiative, be active and passionate creating my vision. I would add the blue triangle with red square (Number 5) to enhance the power of promoting an idea whose time has come. Or, if I want to create material wealth I BALANCE the orange triangle card (Number 3) which again empowers me to attract abundance in all areas of my life.

Balance Centre

TBP is a simple checking and balancing procedure, focusing on the Balance Centre (thymus/heart) which is the bridge between the physical and subtle bodies. This centre balances all of the body's energy

Balance Centre

systems and is intricately linked to every part of us – mind, body and spirit.

All messages that are relayed to and from the brain and the rest of the body are passed via the thymus, for this reason, TBP aims to communicate empowering, life-affirming thoughts and beliefs to the thymus and heart. These positive messages will then be passed on to the brain which will instruct the DNA to influence every every muscle, organ, and cell within the body.

Instructions to check and tune in the TBP Universal Symbol cards:

1. To check if you are in tune with the card: take one card at a time place it on your balance centre with one hand. If you sway forward you are in balance. If you have swayed backwards, left or right or stayed still follow the steps below:
2. Holding the card with two hands on your Balance centre take a deep breath in for a count of nine, hold the breath for a count of nine, as you release your breath think or say Balance.
3. Replace one hand on your balance centre, if you now sway forward you are in balance, however if you are still swaying backwards, sideways or staying still repeat stage 2 until balanced

When you have balanced all nine cards individually place them all in the container and check if you are balanced, as often using all nine cards together can cause a resistance simply balancing all cards together soon clears this.

Summary of the Balance Procedure

TBP is a technique that does not require an understanding of theory or precise disciplines but is learnt through practice. Knowing how it works is not as important as doing it. Rather than using the rational, intellectual level of consciousness, it requires the development of flexibility and expansion of consciousness. It is not the procedure itself, that bring about the results, they are merely catalysts, it is the life force working inside each person that brings about the transformation.

How it works with the mind, body and spirit

- Mind: Placing both hands on your Balance Centre brings your left and right brain hemispheres together, completing the circuit that allows left – right integration of your creation.
- Body: The hand placed on the Balance Centre is naturalistic. You will often see people holding their chest when placed in a situation of shock, trauma or hysterical laughter; it is a way of centring naturally.
- Spirit: By placing your hands on your Balance Centre you are balancing your energy between the physical and spiritual aspects of your being – centring your energies.

The Art of Independence

The red square with the turquoise star symbolises the art of independence and courage- a knowing of who we are, what we want and embodying that. When balanced its energy empowers us to blend the physical and spiritual and eliminating that which is no longer needed for growth. When imbalanced we may be afraid of life, feel like a victim, withdraw from physical reality or operate in our own interests.

A time to focus on the red square energy is when we are matching our passion with our vision or when old ways no longer work for us and we need to get out of our comfort zone and experiment in new ways-a birthing of the new. This energy activates the natural leader and pioneer spirit within us; it is the energy that guides our first steps into anything. Red square energy is fiery and passionate and loves to initiate everything. It is the motivating force within us that pushes us into action with passion to create to our highest potential.

Symbol: SQUARE reflects foundations, stability, physical strength and solidity.

Colour: RED: reflects life energy, the zest and driving force of creation gives power to the strong life qualities of courage, self-confidence , safety and security

Complementary Colour: TURQUOISE: reflects calmness and immunity calms down nervous tension.

Chakra: BASE: reflects our relationship with our physical body and with the material world, it grounds us in physical existence, allowing all our needs to be met. When balanced its energy enables us to blend the physical and the spiritual, eliminating that which is no longer needed for growth.

Number: 1 symbolises the creator and power. A life path one represents independence, determination and strength. You will make your own path in the world be using your ability to think and act for yourself. The spirit of number one is to be able to pass through many different situations and transformations without changing its essence.

In the first year of a nine year cycle, look for new opportunities as it's an excellent time to start a new project or have a new approach to an existing one. Study, plan a career and keep active, this year creates the foundations of the next nine years.

Zodiac Symbols: ARIES: represents our identity and birthing of the new ideas.
CAPRICORN: symbolises wisdom, ambition, loyalty, depth, stability and persistence and a feeling for beauty.

Gem Stones: DIAMOND: inspires creativity, ingenuity inventiveness and brilliance in the world of the 'new'.
RUBY: Passion, self-love

Planetary Influences: MARS: Energy and action self-assertion physical drive, courage, initiative, spontaneity
SATURN: Self-control, logic, security, perseverance

Element Influence: EARTH:Earth seeks straightforward engagement with the physical world, mastery of it through organisation and attainment of abundance, safety and security due to persistence and an efficient sense of timing. Earth is nurturing, dependable, supporting, caring and encouraging.

Physical: Adrenals, skeletal, teeth, hair, legs, feet and nails.

Balanced: Independent, enthusiastic, eager, lives in the present, daring, original strength, energy, vitality, life, sexuality, power alertness and abundance.

Imbalanced: Domineering, arrogant, self-pitying, self-indulgent, quick tempered, impolite, brutal, fear of death, fear of poverty,

Affirmation:

I am independent. I am powerful. I am successful. I am courageous. I am spontaneous. I am strong, and I am energetic. I am life. I am successful. I am a pioneer. I am safe. I am dynamic and passionate. I am fully aware of my position on earth and know all my needs will be met.

The Art of Co-creation

The orange diamond with the indigo star symbolises the art of co-creation, inspiration, desire and passion. When balanced its energy generates joy and has the power to encourage freedom and movement on all levels. It nurtures our creativeness and it enhances our relationships with ourselves and others. When imbalanced we may display or exaggerate our discomfort or distress in order to obtain sympathy or admiration, also known as 'The Martyr Mentality'. This can manifest in sensuality issues as well eating disorders, alcohol abuse, depression and urinary problems

The orange diamond represents the rhythm of life, bringing freedom of movement, strength and passion. It portrays the creation of happiness, a feeling at one with our surroundings and getting closer and more intimate with our partner. Use the orange diamond energy for both worldly power and earthly pleasure; love feeling well and thoroughly enjoy life. It allows the attitude that there is always enough and we will always be provided for. It is comfortable with abundance, and prosperity.

Symbol: DIAMOND creates a dancing experience, having a tendency to 'lift off', flexibility and movement.

Colour: ORANGE reflects joy, movement and creativity and our gut instincts, linking our physical intuition;

Complementary Colour: INDIGO reflects relaxation, peace and expansion. Chakra: SACRAL: A balanced sacral will nurture our creativity and will bring us freedom and enhance our relationships, with ourselves and others.

Number: 2 symbolises the role of the peacemaker and mediator. Two's function best in partnerships or groups, and are willing team players that are diplomatic in handling difficult situations. Two's are co-operative, courteous, considerate and outstanding facilitators and are able to handle situations and people. The second year of the nine year personal cycle is about working with people and being part of a team, building up strong relationships in personal and business areas of your life; realise that it's quality not quantity that counts. Business partnerships are often important too and can grow. So let things come to you naturally as new opportunities can drop in your lap unexpectedly.

Zodiac Symbols:CANCER: symbolises the ability to nurture; having the instinctive and intuitive understanding of the rhythms of nature that bring food to man or the microcosm.
TAURUS: symbolises appreciation and seeing the beauty in everything, feeling abundant and secure.

Gem Stone: Carnelian increases physical energy personal power, creativity and compassion.

Planetary Influences:MOON: represents unconscious mind and the basic body of subconscious human knowledge; internal feelings; gut responses and rhythms.
PLUTO: This planet represents the cycle of life it has powerful links with the conception-birth-death-rebirth cycle in which energy is constantly reborn, dies and is renewed.

Element:WATER: connected with our ability to sense unity through our inner worlds. It cleans and nurtures our physical body so it can grow healthy and beautiful. In the psychological aspect water is our emotions. It is our feeling of life and how this feeling moves us or makes us move: 'e-motion' is energy in motion.

Physical: Gonads, bladder, genitals, kidney, pelvis, body fluids and liquids

Balanced: Enthusiastic, independent, sociable, self-assured, cheerful

Imbalanced: Proud, destructive, exhibitionist, bulimia, misuse of alcohol.

Affirmation:

I am a free spirit. I am imaginative. I am spontaneous. I am fun, I trust my instinctive nature. I am independent. I am flexible, and I am intuitive.

The Art of Clarity

The upward yellow triangle with the violet star symbolises the art of clarity; it is uplifting and inspiring. It encouragers open mindedness and inquisitiveness to explore all possibilities. The triangle directs our attention upwards, as though towards the sun and the attainment of knowledge and wisdom. It is also connected to our personality it transforms the belief 'I can't' to the 'I can'. When balanced the personality's energy gives us clarity of thought, inspirational ideas and increases awareness. Focus on the triangle when you need to be open and spontaneous, authentic and honest. It has a powerful effect on left brain operations such as reading and writing, stimulating the use of words and imagination. The triangle symbol enhances our ability to perceive and understand. When imbalanced you may feel dissatisfied, nervous or tired, are melancholic or a little sad, have weight issues, poor digestion or skin diseases or muscle problems.

Symbol: upright triangle is uplifting and inspiring.

Colour: Yellow is a mental colour, relating to wisdom in thoughts, words and deeds.

Complementary Colour: Violet reflects dignity, divinity, honour value and hope

Chakra: Solar Plexus: is connected to our digestive system and to the physical assimilation of food and its nutrients. Assimilation in the widest sense includes mental psychological digestion of knowledge and experiences.

Number: 3 The number three symbolises creativity, inspiration and embraces the joy of living. Three's follow the path of self-expression and enjoy activities in a harmonious atmosphere. Three is naturally a lucky number and spreads optimism and cheerfulness. Three's are creative and usually enjoy music, writing, singing and acting. They are also imaginative and a joy to be around. Three's have the potential to be powerful public speakers and can effectively inspire and motivate all those around them. They make excellent teachers whether in the home or in the workplace.

The third year of the nine year cycle is a time to expand and develop our creative talents. Seek all forms of self-expression, especially those related to acting, the arts and teaching. This is a great year for socialising meeting friends old and new.

Zodiac Symbol: LEO: Leo is enthusiastic, powerful, expansive and creative, generous and extravagant, assertive and fixed in opinion.

Gem Stones: TIGERS EYE: Solar energy promotes intuitive impressions. AMBER: brings that which is desires to reality.

Planetary Influence: SUN: The centre of our solar system, a star that burns with intense fire and supplies us with light, heat, and energy. In astrology, the Sun is the most powerful planetary influence, bestowing vitality and authority.

Element: FIRE: Fire's essential quality is the energetic exploration of life, to master, to lead and travel both physically and mentally. It is simple and direct in approach and is courageous, energetic and inspirational.

Physical: Pancreas, digestive system, stomach, liver, skin and muscles.

Balanced: enhances cheerfulness, spontaneity and keeps us relaxed and uninhibited.

Imbalanced: loneliness, guilt, psychosomatic illnesses, addictions, pessimistic, sceptical, judgemental, critical, cowardly

Affirmations

I am authentic. I am inspirational. I am optimistic. I am intelligent. I am confident. I am clear. I am aware. I am a learner, and I am honest.

The Art of Love

The green circle with the magenta star symbolises the art of love, the leading principle of life. The circle whose shape embodies the qualities of balance and harmony symbolises equality and freedom. Whichever way the shape is turned it stays the same, constant and forever neutral. It links our physical and non-physical aspects and is our centre of love. It has the power to unite positive and negative energy and transform it into harmony and balance. It motivates us to adapt to continuous change on all levels anchoring our deliberate intention. When balanced we feel at peace with ourselves and others. We are compassionate and are able give and receive. When imbalanced we may be prejudiced, dishonest with money and hold on to possessions.

Symbol: the circle whose shape embodies the qualities of balance and harmony.

Colour: Green is adaptable, understanding, compassionate, generous, harmonic and balancer of the universe.

Complementary Colour: Magenta reflects gentleness warmth and kindness.

Chakra: HEART: The Heart Chakra is the centre of our physical bodies and our spiritual essence; as the heart is the most important organ in our body, love is the core of our being. Through this chakra we relate compassionately and unconditionally with others- with love. Yet this love is not dependent upon others. It is a state of being, and is enduring and constant, regardless of external conditions and circumstances and as ethereal as air. Balanced we experience true self-acceptance. The Heart/Thymus Chakra is the Balance Centre in TBP.

Number: 4 Number four symbolises the organiser and creates security and harmony. It balances work and play. Four builds firm foundations and is efficient and trustworthy. Four is busy and productive. Number four has strong will power and steadfast energy and a reassuring presence. Intuition is the essence of number four's earthly foundations.

A number four personal year is about self-management; loyalty, strength, practicality, steady progress and honesty. Year four creates a firm foundation that can support the maturing of your life goals.

Zodiac Symbol: LIBRA: Libra is motivated by a need to see justice done and will negotiate for equality and inclusiveness of every group represented within a community. Libra seeks balanced exchange in one-to-one partnerships and harmony in groups, using diplomacy and tact to make social efforts more effective. Libra is active, artistic and sociably inclined.
AQUARIUS: Aquarius symbolises advanced thought and is universal in orientation, the sign of hopes and dreams. Aquarius is assertive, progressive, inventive and original It is a promoter of high ideals, valuing scientific and universal truths. Aquarius seeks to transform the culture or community through participation in clubs, groups and organisations. Its intellectual efforts are powered to improve society, driven by a selfless concern that seeks tolerance and full social integration.

Gem Stone: JADE: is known as the 'Sovereign of Harmony'.
EMERALD: The gemstone of prophecy which brings reason and wisdom, uplifts and vitalises; opens to higher states

Planetary Influence: VENUS: Venus symbolises the force of attraction in the universe, bringing things together to form a more perfect, complete and stable whole than that which previously existed in parts. Through Venus we relate to others, appreciate the aesthetic principles of balance, harmony, music, colour and develop co-operation.

Element: AIR: Air is motivated to express thoughts in words to share information, interact with others, and influence society.

Physical: Thymus, heart, arms, hands, lungs, upper back, ribs, circulatory system.

Balanced: Love, joy, unity, kinship and peace.

Imbalanced: Lack of discrimination, jealousy, anger passiveness, anxiety, indifference, stinginess and dishonest with money

Affirmations

I am love. I am spiritual. I am receiving. I am compassionate, I am adaptable and I am generous.

The Art of Communication

The downward turquoise triangle with the red star symbolises the art of communication. It liberates us to communicate our inspired ideas into reality, creating and expanding our future. When balanced we communicate easily and effectively both in verbal and written form. We naturally hone our powers of expression that encourage us to channel our inspired ideas into creative achievements. This energy has the power of promoting an idea whose time has come. It motivates us to moving about both physically and mentally, gathering data and information, learning and studying, communicating viewpoints, sharing advice and opinions moving 'new beginnings' forward.

Symbol: Downward triangle indicates energy focused or channelled downwards from above, moving from one realm to another.

Colour: TURQUOISE: Turquoise is the colour of the sky and the ocean gives us the feeling that life is an endless process. It is connected with sound and voice.

Complementary Colour: RED: Red invites the innovator, one who is tenacious, creative, dynamic, physical life, power, fire and drive

Chakra: THROAT: The throat chakra is associated with our self-expression, communication, wisdom and creativity. It facilitates us to communicate our inspired ideas into reality, creating and expanding our future. When balanced we communicate easily and effectively both in verbal and written form. We naturally hone our powers of expression that encourage us to channel our inspired ideas into creative achievements. When imbalanced we find it difficult to get our point of view across, get a lump in our throats or cry from anger and frustration. We have a fear of change a feeling of being trapped.

Number: 5 Five symbolises adventure resourcefulness and is joyful at heart. It radiates a love of life it is multifaceted and knowledgeable in a wide variety of ways. Fives' knowledge is esoteric and has the authority over things unseen. Number five balances risk and responsibility, and enjoys performing in front of an audience. Fives are versatile, multitalented and inspirational motivators

The fifth year of your personal cycle is about change and variety, being able to get out of a rut and have fun. You will be able to take a new direction with your career or business, doors will open and you will find new solutions for change and growth. The fifth year is associated with social contacts, education, ideas and communication of all kinds.

Zodiac Symbols: GEMINI: Gemini symbolises the duality of the mind, and it integrates the right and left brain function; through the left brain hemisphere it empowers access to the right brain hemisphere; activating intuition, imagination and symbolism. Gemini energy brings extra focus on communication methods which are tools we need to become aware. The more clearly we communicate the better we are understood. Clear communication effects our vitality and ability to be creative.

Speaking, writing, teaching and listening are skills that, when developed, encourage personal growth to know who we are and what we want. Gemini energy is a time of moving about both physically and mentally, gathering data and information, learning and studying, communicating viewpoints sharing advice and opinions to move 'new beginnings' forward.This energy has the power of promoting an idea whose time has come.

VIRGO: Virgo uses its intellect evaluating and organising information clearly, accurately and usefully bringing order out of chaos. Virgo acquires skills and learning leading to our life's work, refining its efforts leading to mastery. It finds security in offering practical dependable service to an organisation or cause.

Gem Stone: TURQUOISE: The turquoise stone induces wisdom and understanding, enhances trust and kindness, mental and spiritual clarity, knowledge, patience, self-expression, and the connection between the body and the mind.

Planetary Influence: MERCURY: This is the planet of communication, intelligence, memory, expression, thinking, talking, learning, and teaching.

Element: ETHER: The most subtle and expansive of the elements, it is everywhere. It is *the space* the other elements fill. The mind is also composed of ether; it is formless and impossible to contain.

Physical: Thyroid, throat, neck, jaw, voice, shoulders arms and hands.

Balanced: inquisitive, entertaining, versatile, liberal and broad minded. Also inventive stimulating, non-judgemental and intuitive.

Imbalanced: Unfocused, scattered, impatient, inconsistent, argumentative, easily bored, impatient and irritable, gossipy, nervous, non-committal manipulative and fickle.

Affirmations

I am creative. I am a pioneer. I am a communicator. I am versatile. I am spontaneous. I am adaptable. I am intellectual, and I am lively.

The Art of Visualisation

The indigo trapezoid with the orange star symbolises the art of visualisation. Using this symbol with intention we can attain greater command of our lives and respond with enhanced awareness and sensitivity to the 'command' of our spirit. It also brings insight, which links perception with understanding. It is related to the act of seeing, both physically and intuitively. When balanced it opens our psychic abilities and our understanding of archetypal identities. It also allows us to see clearly, in effect letting us 'see the whole picture'. When imbalanced we are not able to focus on the job in hand, we lack concentration and have a distorted view point. Physical imbalances can manifest in headaches sinus problems and eye problems, mental confusions, nightmares and absent mindedness.

Symbol: TRAPEZOID: Symbolising levity, the shape is like a chalice. It is ready to move energy, filling and emptying.

Colour: INDIGO: Indigo can see more than can be seen . It symbolises mystical wisdom; self-mastery, communication, profound insights and instant understandings

Complementary Colour: ORANGE: Symbolises our gut instinct linking our intuition – joy, movement, creativity.

Chakra: BROW: The Brow Chakra is associated with our sixth sense (extrasensory perception) a finely tuned awareness, which enhances our imagination, psychic powers, intuitiveness and second sight. When balanced we are able to look into the past and see into the future. We are in control of our lives and have the courage to go with our gut instincts and premonitions. When imbalanced we are unable to concentrate, which can lead to lack of clarity or over analysing situations. Physical imbalances can manifest in the form of visual and sinus problems, headaches and nightmares.

Number: 6 Six symbolises sensitivity compassion harmony and charisma. The number six is the love that unites all of humanity through integration of the masculine and feminine polarities. Number six is magnetic in attracting love, fun and social interaction. Six expresses inner divinity through teaching and guidance. It also symbolises abundance, six flourishes at anything it tries.

The sixth year of your personal cycle strengthens relationships and enables you to build new and lasting friendships. In this sixth year you will be oriented around the home, family and community in a conscious and nurturing way.

Zodiac Symbol: PISCES: Pisces is receptive, intuitive and emotional, imaginative, romantic, impressionable and mystical, adaptable, and very changeable.

Gem Stone: SAPPHIRE: The deep blue stone brings joy and peace to the mind

Planetary Influence: NEPTUNE: Ecstasy, refinement, spirituality, imagination, pure love, and altered consciousness.

Element: Light

Physical: Pineal, pituitary, automatic nervous system, face, nose, ears and eyes

Balanced: Widens our perspective, brings us visionary talents and heightens our powers of intuition and psychic powers.

Imbalanced: Intolerant, impractical, sees only the dark side, and melancholy.

Affirmations

I am a visionary. I am flexible and passionate. I am fully responsible for my thoughts words and actions

The Art of Knowing

The downward violet pentagon with the yellow star symbolises the art of knowing. It pertains to enlightenment, dynamic thought, truth and being at one with the world- a state of bliss. When balanced we appreciate our uniqueness and we have a perfect understanding and union with the universe. Imbalanced we compare ourselves to others or to our internal checklists, which can manifest in negativity, shame, depression and ridged thought patterns.

Physically the downward violet pentagon is linked to our nervous system which can affect mental ability and the psychic potential in every human being. The rays of the pentagon symbolise the five senses in human being, which are also meant for acquiring knowledge, our eyes, ears, nose, tongue, and skin.

In addition, there are five working senses: voice, legs, hands, anus and genitals. Then, there are five objects of the senses: smell, taste, form, touch and sound.

Symbol: Pentagon The pentagon symbolises the five senses in human being, These senses are also meant for acquiring knowledge.

Colour: VIOLET: Violet is a combination of red and blue with red bringing practicality to the undirected expansiveness of the blue, and allowing more creative energy to emerge. Violet is associated with imagination and inspiration.

Complementary Colour: YELLOW: Yellow gives clarity of thought, great ideas and increases awareness.

Chakra: CROWN: The crown chakra is our chakra of consciousness. Physically this chakra is linked to our nervous system, which can affect mental ability and the psychic potential in every human being. Balanced the crown chakra is linked with cosmic energy and is open to all possibilities at a level that abandons intellect to the power of passion experience and 'knowing'

Number: 7 Seven symbolises mysticism and enjoys an amazingly rich inner life. Seven is imaginative and proficient in deep thought, has a powerful open mind with a wealth of original thoughts and creativity. Seven, though an abstract thinker, intellectual, inventive and enigmatic, also enjoys solitude and likes to display knowledge in public.. Finding the underlying answers in everything relating to nature and the meaning of the universe is typical of a seven, who will link the practical to the theoretical and the conventional to the unconventional. Seven posits success, talent and efficiency and is naturally sensitive and is able to assist mankind.

The seventh year of the cycle is about reflection. Reflect on who you are and what you want. Disregard unneeded things. It is a great time to develop interests in metaphysics.

Zodiac Symbol: SAGITTARIUS: Sagittarius is optimistic and freedom-loving, good-humoured and straightforward. Intellectual and philosophical Sagittarius explores the physical realm, through travel, and the mental realm through reading or formal education, to gain knowledge. It pursues philosophy and metaphysics to discover the meaning of life.

Gem Stone: AMETHYST: This is a stone of the mind. It brings calmness and clarity where there is anxiety and confusion. Wear Amethyst if you want to get in touch with your intuition, your feelings, or your values. Amethyst assists one to learn of all things spiritual, mystic and psychic.

Planetary Influence: JUPITER: Expansion and joy, opportunity, luck, abundance, sharing wealth and knowledge.

Element: ALL ELEMENTS

Physical: Hypothalamus, central nervous system and brain

Balanced: Mental strength, inspirational, kindly and just, humanitarian

Imbalanced: Superior, arrogant, snobbish, disloyal, fanatic

Affirmations

I am philosophical. I am stimulating. I am optimistic. I am straightforward. I am free. I am open minded. I am sincere. I am dependable, and I am good-humoured.

The Art of Transformation

The upward magenta pentagon with the green star symbolises the art of transformation. The key to this symbol is the idea of letting go. Use it also where change is needed to let go of old thought patterns or old memories, or when you need to change your daily or weekly routines, needs in food or habitat. Letting go and having faith in the future often implies getting out of a comfort zone and trusting your intuition. It also symbolises regeneration and the beginnings and ends of phases in life- death and resurrection. Imbalanced we can become rigid and static and no longer able to develop and evolve.

Symbol: UPWARD PENTAGON: Symbolises the aspiration to completeness. It is a symbol of perfection in sacred geometry

Colour: MAGENTA: Magenta is majestic. It is a combination of red and violet, and is the colour of 'letting go" allowing change.

Complementary Colour: GREEN: Green is harmonious and soothing.

Chakra: ALTA MAJOR: Located at the back of the head, just above the point where the skull joins the neck, this chakra is linked to the occipital area of the brain, which is, in turn, linked to the optic nerve. It is connected with vision, both spiritually and physically. When the Alta Major Chakra is balanced, it can enable us to see the big picture in life. It enhances intuitive ideas and makes them more solid, tangible and achievable. It gives them form.

Number: 8 Number: 8 In mathematics the symbol of the infinity is known as leminscate ∞, turned ninety degrees, it becomes the number- 8.Eight represents continuation, repetition and eternal spiral motion of cycles. It maintains the balance between material prosperity and spiritual achievement and brings in a plentiful harvest. Number eight shows love and affection freely, is a natural leader, extremely intuitive and able to sum up situations instantaneously.

The number eight personal year is a time to focus on wealth and ways to increase it. You will get recognition for your prior years of performance in an 8 year.

Zodiac Symbol: SCORPIO: Scorpio has depth, strength intensity and determination, and an almost hypnotic powerful passion that can be beneficial when using energy to transform oneself and assist others and the environment..

Gem Stone: ROSE QUARTZ: The 'TheGentle Love' stone. Planetary Influence: URANUS: Originality, genius, curiosity and independence, It rules the sixth sense, intuition and can shift perception.

Element: ALL ELEMENTS

Physical: ETHERIC: Again, ether can be viewed as the state between energy and matter and consists of tiny energy lines similar to the line on a television screen. It is blue print of the physical body and connected to our senses.

The etheric body has three interrelated functions- the receiver, simulator and transmitter of energies. In the human being, each function is maintained in a state of balance; the physical body reflects this as a state of good health. The key to health lies in the correct reception, acceleration and distribution of energies.

Balanced: Determined and forceful, emotional and intuitive, powerful and passionate exciting and magnetic.

Imbalanced: Jealous and resentful, compulsive and obsessive, secretive and obstinate.
